THE GUARDIAN OF THE TOWER

Teresa Briganti

 www.trafford.com

North America & international
toll-free: 1 888 232 4444 (USA & Canada)
phone: 250 383 6864 ♦ fax: 812 355 4082

THE GODESS OF FAIRYLAND

Her presence was felt long before she entered the room.

He said: "my wife will be here soon" and moved away as if he had something on his mind. I sensed the sound of devotion in his voice. He reminded me of the elves of his land. His Irish eyes, two clever pools of greenish brown, could hide any feelings which lingered in his soul. The sea in the cove below roared among the ruins of the ancient monastery that appeared fragile, yet eternal, beyond and above time and space. I admired the scene but then turned to mingle with society. I whirled around the room in a place wonderfully unfamiliar to me where, I thought, I could "rest my soul". I felt at ease in its sober luxury, my dark outfit matching perfectly with the black tablecloth set dramatically on the table.

Everyone seemed to be different from anyone I had ever met before and I could breathe freedom all around. We were all "blown in" as the locals say, blown in by the wind of chance, desire, despair or adventure. We were foreigners who had found peace amidst these rocks between the ocean and the fields trying to call this place home.

Nothing was ordinary in the house where the party was going on and never would be. The walls were not white but "soft hessian", with a dash of "elephant's breathe"; a special color distributed by a posh English company. The kitchen cabinets had been imported from Italy, the window sills from Germany, marble floors from God knows where, and the pink couch from Paris, soft, soft "forget your troubles" pink. Wine glasses were scattered all over the place; it was a house warming party, after all.

Bright red carpets flashed against the pale walls but something seemed to be missing. Silk skirts, jeweled bodies and abundant wine were waiting for her arrival . . . I could hear the ladies whispering her name to one another with admiration. Riding, she has been riding, but she was coming . . . After what seemed a lifetime the door opened, she entered the room, dressed in an understated black outfit embellished only by a silver chain with some sort of Celtic demigod that stared at the crowd. She, "the Goddess of the Island", was simply enchanting, apparently unaware of all the excitement, as she made her way through the room to greet me. "You come from Italy. Wonderful place . . . the colors . . . so vibrant! I love your country."

The instinct of a painter lingered deep in her soul. I felt protected and at ease with her. The wisdom and charm of this lady stood out dramatically and for a long time after that I shined in her light and enjoyed her "joie de vivre" with simplicity. Her blue eyes, a spring of fresh water, many times quenched my thirst for compassion and understanding, until I lost sight of them.

I had to leave again. It was not the place where I could "rest my soul" after all.

TORRE GREGORANA

Now I stand on duty as the guardian of this ruined tower that overlooks the Mediterranean Sea. I've seen so many things going on inside and outside this place. I think "I've seen it all". So there is no purpose in making decisions that could change my life . . . nothing will change.

I'm sitting on the dock of the bay . . . , as the song goes, suspended in the dark on this terrace, overlooking the sea. I perceive from a distance the lighthouse of our neighboring town.

Its beam brings my thoughts back to earth as the sea becomes the stage for a beautiful moon that fills these magic nights of my unique life. The atmosphere is crammed with unspoken words and this ambiguity leads me to breathe in the mystery of the universe and its creation.

I have always abandoned myself to the wind, the ocean waves and the Moon.

Long ago, I made up my mind, left everything behind, never to return, directed thoughts to where I could begin "breathing "anew. Since then, I have lived several other lives in different places with the same purpose. But they are all the same, in the end. Why should I want a new dress? Where am going?

Indeed, I might find the right occasion to wear a new robe, go out into the street, and face some odd lady and say: "Yes, I know perfectly what I am going to do in the future. I know my purpose in life. Damn it if I know!"

The lady dressed in blue and white would smile at me as I changed my mind over and over again.

Perhaps, I should wait until this afternoon to decide.

The air is fresher and the cooler breeze gives more perspective to dreams. Then, when evening comes I will ask myself "Why should I begin a new project, no purpose, let's just go to bed . . . tomorrow."

I am the Guardian of the Tower where everything has already happened.

History has repeated itself so many times in this place I call home . . . How can I expect novelties? plans? What hopes? I am to protect and defend Greg but with what energy, if I can barely handle myself?

Gregoriana, the tower, is a wrecked beauty, like me, all wrinkles and holes. We are proud of both; it took us so much pain to get them. She was mined during World War II and has never recovered; a reminder of human folly as I am of foolishness and we get along perfectly together.

We know the faults and tricks of history and of our next door neighbor. We do not trust anyone, not even ourselves. All is lost except the end.

Yet the sun comes out each morning in the promise of a glorious day and I cannot pull out from this game. I go on with the illusion of beauty that so many times has deceived me . . . once more.

BEAUTY AND PAIN

One morning, it must have been around eight o'clock as the liner from Ponza, always on time, was moving out of the port, the doorbell rang and in she came.

Tall, tanned, out of a Vogue magazine, she grabbed a chair, sat at the table and with her beautiful green eyes looked straight into mine; night swallowed nearsighted dots in an empty face.

She sat still and asked me to listen. For once she needed me. It had to be dam important if she had moved from her white castle to reach my ruined tower instead of heading for the beach on such a magnificent day.

While I went on with my selfish, skeptical thoughts, she burst into tears, and believe me it was completely another story. Her sadness swept through the air of the open garden, ran over the waves down below and hit cold my heart.

"What's the matter?" I asked. No answer, not even one sound came out of that creature all shivers and pain. Yes, I know that feeling; so miserable words cannot express the deep pain inside . . . understanding . . . no words.

My thought went back to the year before, the rain pouring over the house, over the grey blue water beneath the cliffs. I could see the water, edging up the rocks from down below, rising to chase the dust along the road, the deafening sound confounding my baffled thoughts and I said to myself: "why should I bother?" I looked outside and all I could see was my reflection on the window pane, my mind its only companion.

After a while she came into the room and stared at me without emotion. Her hair was stylishly done and her makeup perfect to the point it was out of place in such circumstances.

But her heart was gone, her voice was miles away . . . distant to our mortal hearts. It was gone forever; she had lost her gorgeous boy in a motorcycle accident and had lost her mind.

Then I knew, she could laugh and talk about the new show in town, but I had lost her just as she had lost her beloved . . . I wished I were an artist with a heart not so empty, so I could bring some consolation.

For once, only for a few seconds, I forgot my boring hysterical self and really wished I could help.

It lasted but for a few seconds. Why should I get involved in something I am not able to handle? Pain and sorrow. I think I've had my share.

Now, as you sit in front of me, do not kindle my sense of guilt, do not be obsessed and let me love you the way I can. We have both had our lot of grief. It is part of growing up.

I lost my country at ten, my father at twenty. Left alone with my mother and married immature,

I still carry the burden of irresponsible decisions for the rest of my so-called life.

She had lost her son a few months before and was trying to cope with life day by day.

That morning, for some reason, the pills she was taking could not help to ease the pain. "Help"

I thought I heard her say. How could I help her? "Change brand of pills", I cynically wanted to reply, but the words would not come out.

I recalled all the times I needed help, up to yesterday . . . no one there, no one to watch over me.

So I took her hand, leaned her forehead against my shoulder and caressed her hair. There isn't much else you can do against life. A shoulder to lean on does miracles. But it is hard to find.

Many, many years ago, I lost my dad and the world collapsed over me. She would come each morning, find her way through my floating, drowning soul and would feed me small pieces of fruit because I had lost any notion of hunger, thirst or feelings in general . . . . It helped, not the food, but

I could feel her love for me and that was what I needed. Love is so hard to find.

So this time she could feel me reciprocating and little by little, I could sense her soul arising from the depths . . .

After a while, she was herself again, ready to play her part in this crazy world where one must always shine, no matter what. She left smiling and another day was made.

Nothing else happened that day except for the rain, the seagulls and the boat back from Ponza on schedule, like countless days before.

But my heart dimly perceived what had "really" happened that morning.

For once I had "given" love or whatever you call it.

SOCIAL LIFE AND MOTHERHOOD

The tower and I are good companions. On some special occasions we "dress" with wild flowers, put on a show and play the fashionable hosts.

The courtyard is filled with flowers; their perfume mixes with the smell of the sea down below, whining at the dark. Candles and spotlights brighten the darkness in spite of my budget concerned husband.

A buffet is set with my Vietri collection, vivid blue and sparkling yellow, mingled harmoniously with soft turquoise and deep burgundy. Our guests arrive and, if it is their first time, they stare speechless, overwhelmed by the beauty of the place.

Gregoriana and I watch carefully their amazed and envious expression. We rejoice and sometimes experience a shivering fear.

Envy is threatening and I am to guard this beauty given to me by God, nature and my parents' wallet.

After our guests recover from their surprise, their attention is drawn towards the tower they have heard so much about. So she gets her well deserved moment of glory.

". . . . yes it was the pearl of the Pope's defense system in the 1600s against the Turks; no enemy could go by this place and survive. It is a pity; the most beautiful of the towers had such an unlucky Fate."

It was built in 1587 as a protected fortress against the Turks and was destroyed by the Germans in World War II.

It could have been any war, or time, or place; no difference. History only repeats itself and human soul never changes. A ruin now, she remains a magnificent memento . . . if that is of any use. "What a beauty, what a shame." It is always the same old story, same old scene.

"Please help yourself to the buffet, Today we have a generous catch from our fisherman.

Taste this wine, isn't it wonderful? "Alla salute" . . . and there you go another day to bury.

My thought goes to my mom, as usual when I go to bed. She has gone, my mother, with her advice, her anxiety, her love. She has nothing to worry about anymore.

The sun has gone down and it is getting cold. The golden sun has made love to the blue waves all day long and now it needs some rest.

My soul and my body are tired too. Thank God they have all left. The show is over and hopefully

I will have a good night sleep.

Look! There is a fish jumping above the water and swimming towards our rock! . . . . Great . . . Good night.

WHITE TULIPS

Dull November day . . . the streets of Rome
Faces and places I did not see and yet I will
    never forget.
White flowers for your birthday . . . for your
    funeral
I could not know
Like a child you smiled at your birthday present
    before going away
I could not stop you . . . . you had to go.
You left those flowers behind and brought me
    with you.

She has gone but I can feel her presence around me, the warmth of her love.

I, a mother of three do not think I can even vaguely describe the love I have for them. The only thing that keeps this little life in me going is their existence . . . The fire that still burns in my heart is for them . . . But soon it will go. I don't think it ever will completely . . . I will be the guardian of the tower for them. You tower over there, as wrecked as you are, you will be here when I am gone . . . you must help me watch over them.

Dear Boys, think of me as a dream, not a nightmare, only a dream. Dreams are made of air and as the weather changes so does my heart. I am like the wind, always have been, and like the air the wind is made of, I too shall blow away one day.

But I will not leave you. I will be in the summer breeze that blows through your hair at sunset on the sea or among the leaves on a warm summer afternoon. I will be there to watch over you and you will not be alone.

BRUNETTE AND LONELY

Gregoriana kept looking for my friend all summer. She would always call in at the beginning of the season, husband in hand, along with sun bathing gears and a handful of shopping bags with food for an army "just for a little lunch." We would sit all day long chatting and gossiping away. When lunch time would come, sitting in the shade; the three of us would enjoy a fine glass of wine, commenting on the sugar daddies in their yachts anchored in front of us.

Blissful days! Brunette and athletic, marked by years and inevitable tears, she would always come and sunbathe on the terrace. It was so relaxing here with Gregoriana and me.

She would let herself go and forget her grumbling husband watching her in the corner. Her young age had brought to her the difficulties of a lonely marriage.

Together, less alone, we would share the pain of our present condition; husbands like walking shadows, our boys gone abroad trying to find a decent life that this country has always refused to give younger generations not politically connected. Sex drugs and alcohol, nothing else.

"Italia Paese di poeti santi e navigatori . . ." I wonder who said that.

Unemployment in Italy has always been notoriously high. Our young, educated people must hang around pubs, tabernas, cerverias, sklepas, bars of the world, looking for a better life.

We would make the same comments exchanging the same views on the matter, and then we would fall asleep in the song of the sea lullabies, kissed by the loving sun. I enjoyed her company;

She was courageous and down to earth as much as I am hysterical and inconsistent.

But no sign of her this year . . .

No, dear tower you are not the only one to be mysterious. You are the offspring of a rich and noble past, conceived by a King and a Pope to protect the country against Turkish assaults. Queen of the sea and of the Appian Way, immortal against bombs and mines, against violence perpetrated outside and inside, you should know that human heart is cruel and incomprehensible.

But perhaps, you cannot stoop to notice us, the fragile beings that we are, made of stupid thoughts and ridiculous actions. So you are unable to understand when I say that jealousy has taken the mind and heart of her husband. She cannot move, nor live except for the life he allows her.

Love, should not be depriving. It should give joy, hope, courage and similar positive emotions

But as far as I know love is selfish, greedy, and violent.

He treats her like a queen in his foolish attempts to bring back the past; pathetic illusions confuse his mind.

I've lost my dearest friend, someone I would call on when in need of advice, comfort or protection. She is gone. She is gone in spirit, replaced by "happiness" pills where the world becomes a magical merry-go-round leaving her dizzy and wondering if it will ever stop. She takes the pills to relieve the pain of living with the hope it will help.

I am a master at this and doubt it will be any good

Life is a strong, violent force that you cannot control. Folly seems to be one of its most natural components. You can only hide, or pretend to be alright. Perhaps it is because the truth of your reality at this age is finally catching up with you. Previously you may have relied on your creative fantasies to bring you out of such slumps. Now you feel shoved up against the wall with no way to escape.

Accepting the truth may be the only way. We would need compassion for ourselves and others.

We are all on the same boat. but we are too proud to ask.

I love people who, with their heavy burden in life, try to find some relief in our world. Yet it is an illusion. I feel sorry for them

When needed, I try to lend a hand to those who knock at my door. Nevertheless, what I have done for others means absolutely nothing to them. I tried to give without receiving anything in return. I've had enough!

The sun is getting hot. I forgot my sun lotion and the reflection of me in the water proves

I've gained weight. Well, it is too hot. I'll go inside, take a shower then get dinner going.

What do you think Gregoriana? Remember you are my only friend, to advise, to comfort me and all that jazz . . . by the way, Greg, remember we are having company tonight. Try to wear your solemn, mysterious, somewhat gloomy look; it is very effective. In the meanwhile, I shall get ready for tonight. I need some networking.

It is not time to talk about what most bothers our heart. You know that there will be a time to face the problem that keeps my head confused and distracted.

AN OLD CHILD

An only, lonely child,

American childhood disappearing from across the sea . . . Loss.

Italy, unknown places, unknown faces, a language I had always known.

Time to learn and to understand.

Teenager in the Eternal City, aware of Dad's mortality . . . Loss.

The Italian sun could not keep me warm.

College, brilliant graduation, job, marriage all too sudden, all too close, to fill the void inside.

Three angels from heaven sent to an unworthy mother, altogether learning the meaning of motherhood

Mom, my teacher, left me while I was still taking lessons.

I've never learned and never will . . . Loss.

Waves banging against my door, a lullaby to fill my lonely hours.

Future plans of distant countries, to mend deeper wounds

Years of work to come away

Many memories . . . much pain.
My present is already future past . . . Loss.
I still have found nothing to replace what has gone, I
    never will.
Where is my home? It is lost.

THE LABEL

We all must have a label . . . I need one. Where do I belong? Who do I belong to? Uprooted tree in the midst of the storm. What should I wear? I am tired of the neutral colors, sober and refined. But I cannot turn back to my hippy flowery outfits. My dilemma. I used to have long wavy red hair that was perfect with the hippy style. I doubt that my blonde/gray highlights on my medium to short hair would be the same. Life and age do make the difference.

Creativity has gone and boredom has taken its place . . . . what is the color for boredom? (Actually a friend noticed that my interior decoration is boringly elegant). I'll find something "boringly elegant" to wear tonight . . .

One day, three years ago, looking at my son, cans of beer all over the place, bewildered, listening to his harsh words, I thought I heard him say "Get out of here".

I felt that time had come to die as a mother to the world and to myself. I saw hatred in his eyes and I knew that once again I had failed I had reversed on my boy my frustration, guilt and I needed to be forgiven. I felt I had to punish myself and I thought that cutting my beautiful hair would have made me feel better (worse).

I had always been proud of it. Wavy enough to curl over my forehead, I would arrange fantastic flowers over my brows. Red, auburn red. My point of seduction . . .

Time had come I should give up whatever life had meant to me up to then.

It was night time, I got up, grabbed a pair of scissors and got it over with . . . no more lovely lady, socially involved professional, mother etc, just an old hag as hag as possible. I have lost the sparkle in my eyes ever since; two hanging bags is what is left, instead, hardly any expression, addiction to sleep.

My body lies in the sun but my spirit has gone long ago. I have left it on the green hills of Ireland. So what difference should it make what I look like.

My boys are not here; there is no one to please. They are pleased where they are.

Beauty and I are two separate things. No adventure to share no aspiration in common.

I had to start with my hair, the most beautiful part of me. I felt washed away. At first I felt free, invisible.

I got rid of my hair and my old identity but there was no substitution . . . I had overlooked that.

I still do not have a new self. Sometimes I wouldn't mind having one, a bird or a flower would do.

Yesterday at a wacky yoga session someone said "imagine you are a flower". A flower, fresh, smell, sweet shade of creation. I don't know if I would like that.

Live the present . . . Will you, my lovely tower? Forget the past and mind the future for my boys and

Me, while I inhale my reality in one deep breath and free my spirit.

THE WRITER

This time our guest is a famous writer, at least famous around here. I might get some ideas.

She has changed husband/lover so many times, and they all seem to still love her so dearly. Folly.

They say she is lesbian, but nowadays it is so fashionable that you have to watch and beware. There are so many fake gays of all sorts. As long as her talent is good, I have no interests for her preferences in bed . . .

Evening glow confuses my mind. The lights from the towns along the bay reflect their colors blue and yellow on the dark water and it feels like Fantasyland where dreams come true.

Every beautiful thing is possible and there is no pain . . .

But I have seen the old Footman with his wicked sickle, not far away, no use fooling around.

Many have gone before me and I shall go. Greg, you are immortal, you cannot understand, my dear. I am no courageous warrior on the battlefield. I am only the guardian of the tower where a party is going on tonight. The lights on the bay mirror the lights of our house lit up for the occasion.

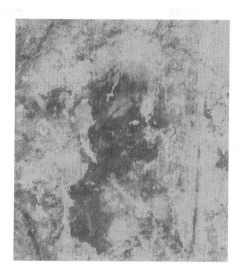

Greg has all her flowers in perfect shape, the stones looking so captivatingly old and meaningful.

The recently discovered fresco is under the spotlight, in the right place, the star of the evening. It is the new attraction.

I often stop and think of this handsome, chained Turkish warrior staring at me while I am in the garden. What is his story? Illusion, faith loss and despair

We all have a story to tell and one to hide. The same script.

The history professor from our local college, the writer's new love, is explaining how Torre Gregoriana (that is her full name) was built in the 16 century as the pearl of the pontifical fortifications on the Tyrrhenian coast to control the Turks. The towers communicated with one another through smoke signals; warning of danger.

Greg why is it that you do not send me signals of danger when needed? Would it help? You could nothing against the insanity of the Germans who mined your heart before leaving.

Lovely young ladies (missed their names) strolling along the garden enjoy the warm breeze while sipping a glass of wine and commenting on how handsome the speaker was.

The smell of their expensive perfume fills the air. Do you realize dear girls that we have been talking about history: victories and defeats, suffering and death of generations of people?

You seem to be so distant from the perception of these matters.

Sensuality and need of physical satisfaction is appalling. (The evening is very "sexy" with the candles, sea breeze, lights and perfumes.)

Life is an illusion and Death is the reality with other events in between. Am I quoting from somewhere?

After her speech the noted writer, dressed in grey with make up as perfect as newly set icing on a birthday cake, makes her way through the crowd and comes to greet me. (Her hair is grey as mine), fifty two, I reckon, goes to the spa at least once a week.

She is wearing Armani grey . . . I never wear Armani . . . I will never become a famous writer. Rumors of adoring, past lovers abound and one wonders, how and why for someone who betrayed them all . . . I don't even see friendship/ sympathy from my companion to whom I've been true all my life.

Perhaps I am too boring.

She shook my hand and complimented me on the nice evening and beautiful place.

Well, after all, I thought, I am the guardian of the tower. I spent all my money on this place.

Gregoriana is my only girl. She is a military fortification but I think of her as a girl because she knows suffering in body and "soul" as only a woman does. The lights turned brighter as the sky became darker.

Down below, in the water in a little "gozo" a couple was making love . . . laughter and then no sound at all.

THE MERMAID DREAMER

I saw him in a distance, his bald head reflecting the moonlight. Steady in his pace and shaky in his hands, he was still handsome. His senses had chilled long ago, but his mind was wide awake while grabbing a very unstable chair near my forgotten Jacuzzi. He showed his age when he sat down

His knees; his problem were his knees. At the age of 82, life was all in the ups and downs of his knees. Elegant posture mirrored his aristocratic background restrained by trifles such as pain!

In his early days he had seen the tower standing bold and invincible. Like himself, ready to defend and conquer the world. But years had gone by, he had seen so much, was tired and would have rather skipped the conversation.

He had loved and married; illusions of a young man of twenty two at the turn of the century. His love was fair and his love was true. His life; he was willing to dedicate his life to his wife and their little boy.

One day an officer from a distant town stopped by to visit the city. Mary, (that was his wife's name) was at the café' with her friend. Her blue dress suited her perfectly. Her fair complexion and her blue eyes did the rest.

It was love (?) at first sight. He saw her and she looked into his soul, no more strangers but lovers forever, until it lasted.

So she left her husband and their child for this new dream dressed in a uniform. Months went by and she gave no sign, no letter to her son, none to her husband . . .

One day they found her outside their door simple and sober as ever, lovely of a beauty made of different shades of pain, a smile, not the girlish smile anymore. No one asked and she gave no explanations.

He looked into her eyes but could not see. He was blind, frustration and disillusion had tortured him for too long. No words, not even fierce ones. A few days later she received a letter in which he was giving her instructions; she was to leave the house immediately with the child. There would have been a small apartment in the centre of town for her, their son and her father.

Her husband would have taken care of all the expenses but she had been banned forever from his heart.

Love and pride, don't work together. I, the guardian of the tower where nothing happens, I gazed into his eyes while he was sitting on a chair looking over the sea and saw the truth: pain, memory and love that time cannot consume. He was calm, relaxed but I knew then and there that his wife had died to him long before her actual death, long ago, yet his pain was still alive and overwhelming.

He had lived his youth dreaming of the mermaids on the bottom of the sea that had filled his childhood illusions.

False truths had made up his dreams. Reality is a different story, brutal and ruthless, too much to bear.

So he decided to die to himself and what we were looking at was the empty image of an elderly gentleman, aware of the truth of our existence.

He could not forgive life for having deceived him so badly. There was anger in those eyes that seemed to look afar.

Why do people come here to find peace?

The tower and I, wrecked ruins of existence living on what life spared us are of no help.

Greg keeps playing her role of the historical site of great importance.

I, The Guardian of the Tower have my share of despair, deep dark moments of nonexistence.

The lullaby of the sea in its eternal coming and going . . . . going . . . without return no more pain, regret, guilt feelings. Down in the bottom of the sea where the mermaids would sing to me and friendly fish would keep me company, no more darkness, no harmful monster and, pain gone forever.

Our moment of glory has passed, and we have missed it. There is no hope it will return again. We would not be prepared. We have lost our ambition, our lust for fame.

There is peace here, the battle is over. The Turks and German have vanished and so have the Chinese.

The fighting is over here but outside the struggle gets worse each day.

OUR NEIGHBOR

Our neighbour lives on the other side of the street and yet seems to be living thousands of miles away, on the other side of the universe. Her movements are always slow as if the effort of her existence has taken up all her energies and there isn't much left to rely on.

Her dress depends upon her mood, unpleasant most of the time . . . gone has she from herself so many times that it gets harder and harder for her to recognize her being and "get together" ready to face the day.

She would often come over in the warm summer afternoons for a cup of coffee and some gossip

There was no story about violence and abuse that she was not familiar with.

The shawl she wore would slip over her shoulder and she would quickly put it back into place as if someone had seen her totally naked. She seemed to be afraid of everything and yet has always had the courage to stand up to her husband and his violence over her.

More than once she had been taken to the hospital because of the injuries. Headaches, vertigos, panic attacks were the consequences but she would never give up and let him put an end to that pseudo—life of hers. On the other hand she would not leave, set herself free.

It was her real fault and she needed to be punished; Staying was her due punishment. Perhaps it would mean admitting another failure, the worse of all.

Money, his struggle and greed for money was unbearable.

She knew the bitterness of living with a man that she once thought would be the man of her life and realizing that she had been terribly wrong. Once the truth is revealed you die inside, and so did she.

Relatively young (fifty five), she had seen all her dreams crushed up and thrown into the waste basket and nothing to nourish her soul except hatred, regret and anger, a constant battle and no end in sight . . . clear signal that the load of responsibility was heavy, more than a fair share. "Yes, I love the boys . . . money for them . . . trying to find a job for them . . . who will they meet . . . who will take care of them when I am gone."

The possibility of being blamed would always be present and her sense of guilt and failure was daily bread to nourish her bad feelings.

That evening she ran across the street and came to my gate, calling me out loud, expecting no answer since it was rather late.

Late but beautiful.

The full moon was out dancing her magic dance of nonsense over the bewildered water that stood still and watched the show. We were both enchanted . . .

It is hard for me to go to bed when the full moon is out on a summer night. It is as if a whole new world opens to your senses, to your soul and you are totally carried away from your sorrows and pains. I sit there all alone and yell at the moon. Coyote.

As soon as I opened the gate that night, she rushed in "Did you hear the news on TV? A man on trial for spousal abuse declared innocent because his wife was stubborn and would not change her behavior.

She was condemned in other words for being strong, for standing up and not giving in to male dominance, she was punished . . ." she said and adding "after all I punish myself daily in the lack of courage to leave and kill myself slowly by staying."

ETERNAL LOVE UNDER THE SUMMER SUN

The heat, unbearable and fierce tarnished my sight and my thoughts, no place for anything other than "breathe" . . . the boats down below had become uncountable, too many as the day went by and I needed air.

I felt the urge to leave the tower, go away even if only for a drive along the city's main street. Sales on and the crowd getting more packed at ever corner. A bright, multifaceted, senseless, stream of people in a useless search of satisfaction. The colors of the items on sale in the shops flashed like lighting against the shopping window and reflected the light of the sun which invaded the streets and raged pitiless over the crowd who simply ignored their Fate, caught in the trap of consumerism.

Shopping, buying new clothes; as if it helps to change existence . . . fools.

I hate sales so I knew that I was there only because of my confused mind and more confused soul.

I tried to get away from there as soon as possible and began to run along the alleys that bring straight to the beach . . . crammed space dotted by colorful umbrellas apparently protecting happy people slowly roasting under the sun. The colors were lit up by the violent rays of a remorseless sun: afternoon at the sea on a summer Sunday. Music; loud and endless music; the same old song over and over again. No one listening, so it made no difference. They really needed noise to fill their empty minds as the objective was to lay still and get a perfect suntan. The smell of the many brands of sun lotion reached my nostril and made me sick.

Gradually, feeling the desperate shove towards freedom, I found myself on the rocks in another part of town. Rocks again; fresh, cool rocks, no shade but no need for it since the waves kept me cool.

At last I sat and relaxed, no one to bother me, no people. I am starting to be fed up with people. I have lost my habit to interacting, communicating. I live with silence as my companion, interrupted by yelling and shouting, then silence again, thick silence that covers the world, your soul, your mind. While everything becomes one huge mess with you standing in the middle, unaware, not knowing what's next . . .

"Excuse me, madam"; silence interrupted.

I looked up and perceived very dimly an elderly man with a great smile on his face. Wearing tennis shoes and a camera in his hands, I knew he was one of the hundreds of tourists that invade our town ever weekend, especially in summer.

However there was something about him that attracted my attention and awakened my curiosity. So I tended my ear to his words as he handed me his high tech camera" Could you please do a little video of my wife and I as we walk along the beach?"

Wife? I looked further behind his shoulders and there she was his wife.

A dear old lady perhaps eighty years old, dressed in blue with a big straw hat on her grey hair tied in a knot: lovely lady, blue sweet eyes, used to surrender and acceptance. Straight in her posture, sweet in her smile she carried a few seashells in her small hand.

I accepted at once touched by the romantic idea of the two, still young at heart. So I followed them with their camera as they walked along the beach, played with the waves, collected seashells.

I was so happy to see that love had still space in their lives, no matter what my situation could be.

I saw hope in them for my not distant future.

I kept following them with the joy of a child chasing a bird with a new given camera. I felt it was a moment to cherish. Yes, they were together, they were happy together . . . maybe someday

I could . . . But time came to an end. The elderly man turned around as if to say that it was enough.

I gave him his camera and I smiled pleased at what I thought was an image of love and devotion.

I could hardly believe his words as I leaned towards him. "So, I can send it to our daughter who lives far away and show her we have not split up yet". He did not smile and was unbearably serious.

He thanked me and went away followed by his wife who could hardly keep up with his pace. So being left behind, she decided to sit on a rock nearby, alone. Her slow but steady movements proved to me that she was used to it . . . that was her way of life, all she had. There was a sweet sadness in her eyes while she stared at the blue and seemed thought free . . . her husband sat on the bench in the corner and opened up a newspaper without even looking at her,.

That was more than I could bear; I turned around crying and ran as fast as I could back to my car. I drove like mad until I got back; inside the black of my old prison on the sea. Why was I so stupid to believe there could be something to look forward to, at my age, another illusion. I will never learn.

I just couldn't get rid of the sting of disappointment ferociously burning inside; no hope, no hope for me tomorrow.

I rushed to the kitchen cabinet and reached out for my happiness pills, that, by the way, hardly create the illusion of joy in me anymore.

AN UNWRAPPED GIFT

On a glorious morning like this it is hard to say "God does not exist" I sense His presence in the sun coming up from yonder hills, replacing the magic moon. This eternal dilemma: the sun and the moon. It is the light in both of them that does the trick. Light is life to me. Its reflection on the wavy water sliding southwards is a cascade of fireworks on this day the fourth of July . . .

Negative thoughts do not even dare come to my mind in such an ecstasy

My only companion, the old Footman himself, can sit rest and enjoy the show, until my hour comes.

Light of the newborn day, shines on everything created, "it shines on the rich as on the poor";

I heard that somewhere. It is rather obvious, but effective. Yes, it shines on my oleanders, cactus, and palm trees as well as on the weeds making them look just as glorious and unique . . . God's creatures.

Life is a gift unexpected, unwrapped. We often spend our whole life holding this box in our hands, we mistreat it, throwing it here and there and sometimes even throwing it away. We never stop to open it

I wonder will I ever have the courage to lift the lid.

Gregoriana has awakened to the sun, her worn out terracotta bricks shine like gold and she is beautiful too.

"What do you think about the unwrapped gift, my dear?" . . .

"Crap" is the answer. (military jargon)

THE STORM

My son is here . . . I have nothing to give; nothing for his soul nor for his future.

I don't know what will be, but now on such a morning, I just can't be bothered.

That Wednesday, around three o'clock, the sky turned black and the phone rang.

The sea was motionless, colorless when it began to swirl in all directions until the waves from miles to the west began to move towards our rock. The wind started blowing and blowing hard as if it would get rid of all the scrap, as if God thought there was a need for cleaning up.

I collected what I could of the leftovers. Gregoriana had dozed away, but now she was awaking. She had sat in the sun all day and was excited for the refreshing shower that was arriving.

I ran into the house just before it started pouring. Lucky, There is no need to water the plants . . .

I remember when my son was a small child, he was afraid of storms. "My son should not grow up with fears" I thought. So I once I made up a tale for him about angels watering the plants of our world to make it more beautiful. Thus explaining what a storm was . . . a lie for sure. But to me, with him so small and innocent standing besides, "that" was the truth and he trusted me.

A world of make believe was the only reality I had for both of us . . . It was wonderful. He believed me I could see the fear in his eyes subside. Yes, he would have never been afraid.

I would have protected him . . . finding the courage in some hidden corner of my fragile soul.

I was wrong. How could I know? No one had taught me to be a mother. Nor to be an adult.

I was taking life experiences away from him and in time he hated me for this.

The wind was pounding hard against my heart as he left for good. The house sounded empty, the wind shouting behind shut doors.

Ghosts only ghosts. I live in a house full of ghosts, where the wind blows through the windows and the rain finds its way along the cracks in the walls. I have no place to go, nor the will to dream anymore.

I have tried hard to keep the grip on this mountain climb that we call life. But it is slippery and I am growing weak. I will fall sooner or later. I will fall in relief. Why should I keep trying?

The next day no sign of the storm, the sun was shining and the sea had forgotten its rage.

THE LOVELY BUSINESS LADY

She entered the gate without ringing the bell. I was expecting her.

She had called and said she was arriving from Dublin on the first plane she could get.

Her hair. Despite her age, her hair was still seductive red and her smile a promise of paradise. Her deep blue eyes looked around checking every corner until they stopped at the sight of the sea, staring at it as if to challenge which blue was bluer. Uninvited, she sat at the table and joined us for breakfast.

She had always been criticized and ill labeled in her ability to make life go her way.

She lived on her own, without a man, with many men, against one man in times in which such behavior was socially unacceptable in an "honest" lady. She turned her lovely head, shook her hair and began her confession.

Words streamed directly from her heart into the sea below as if he could collect the emotions and carry them far away liberating her heart.

"I have often felt the twinge of inner conflict when I longed for freedom and independence.

Yet I sensed that my heart would have required the security of a close partnership.

But I had none (he was always drunk) So I coped with a monster bigger than myself, fed with hatred, regret anger until it grew so big that I could not compromised any longer.

I was clear and decisive about whatever action to undertake; I walked out of the house when everyone was asleep and left my two girls with their drunken but wealthy father. I had nothing to offer."

She left in her nightgown many years ago and is a wealthy business woman today.

She asked me if she could stay to enjoy the sun and the moon.

She knew how refreshing it was to bathe one's body in both knowing that things would be different in. her spirit when she went away. Her words, poured into the ear of the sea, had gone afar.

Her sensuality and sense of freedom gave new light to our world: she was of the present, without compromise, alive and victim of our times. Whereas I would avoid any decision making . . .

There is too much effort in taking responsibility for our actions: better no action at all . . . we will think about it tomorrow.

I got up this morning before the sun did. There was this pink/blue fresh color in the sky that you would think it is the first day of creation and you are lucky to be there.

The fishermen passing by in their boats waved at me, the Guardian of the Tower.

In the past the guardian had power of life and death over the locals, just like my colleague, the Footman.

I can hear the sound of the old boat of a solitary fisherman, passing under my window

I look out. There used to be a wife with him but now he is alone. The Footman has done his job . . .

Thoughts come and go; nothing seems real at this time of the day . . . better wait after coffee.

BLUE FLOWERS

Blue flowers outside my window
Yellow flowers at my door.
Blue thoughts inside my heart
I will see you no more
No more, no more. no more
The sea knows the truth
No more
The rain cannot tell lies, my soul has no roots
Grey is getting greyer, darkness is too hard to bear
Tell me deep blue sea where shall I go, where?
Where will I see you again?
Along the road to nowhere
Along the path to hell,
You smile at me, stranger without a name.
I know the evil behind you face
The dull expression of your eyes.
Don't look, because you cannot see
Don't try, you will never understand.
Darkness is around, silence is inside
Never thought to find you on my way to hell.
Where shall I hide from your madness?

The Guardian of the Tower

You will find me, haunt me . . .
Will I ever forget those rotten leaves, and rotten souls?
The light is gone . . . you've turned it off.
Yes, better wait for coffee

CONFLICTS

The early morning surprised me with its unbearable heat. My head was pounding hard and only one thought filled my mind and my whole being. Greg in this hot weather you are a special comfort to me. I can sit beneath your walls and feel the freshness of your soul . . . eternally wise. You teach me "To care and not to care."

The young man who came last night (my son) is the light of my life, but there is no way he will ever know it. When I speak to him words go in a different direction from what I'd want to say. I am aware that he will hate me after I die, thinking that it is right and then feeling guilty.

He has never known me because I have never spoken with the words of the heart . . . confusion, loss again and forever. But he should know that when he is around all the beautiful things of my past soar from the deep hidden corners of my soul . . . where I thought there is nothing. They fill my heart with light and joy . . . no more emptiness.

Greg we have lost so many things yet the past is all that remains. I see my child here and yet

I know he is "gone" into the world, no longer mine. Why should I care?

Children are only lent to us. Greg, childless, sterile old bitch, you are and will remain a child forever, a work of art, and a creature of your creator.

The yachts in front of us keep passing by, without a care in this world, trying to escape the heat of a fierce Italian summer.

Your shelter gives me peace and the past returns to life. I have given you new life. You are my dear creature.

FAITH AND DESPAIR

There had been so much talking about her, long before we actually met and long before I could catch her name and repeat it. She wore a veil, was a very devout Muslim, strong in her faith, well mannered and polite. I saw her and liked her at once. Now I miss her. Sensitive and lively she has left me empty hearted after filling it with feelings of faith, prayer and hope. She would look out on the bay and pray, certain that her God was there to listen and would give her guidance and protection and love. Serenity. Faith gives that feeling of fulfillment of positive trust in existence.

She belonged to a wonderful world not meant for me, no matter how hard I try. I deal with other issues.

Drinking without a purpose . . . if there is a purpose in drinking. Sad, as sad as death on a November day.

My heart shivers and shakes and has nowhere to hide, no escape . . . Leaving is not as easy as simply going away.

My past would follow me; I would be alone with the ghosts of my regrets, my lack of courage, my despair.

Despair, have you ever thought of the dreadful depth of its meaning: no hope, no future, and no chance. The sun is rising like every other day; pure brand new promise of beauty and love which will be disenchanted as the hours go by.

Evening will come and snick behind your shoulders with the tangling pain of another failure, one day closer to your total wreck.

The sun, my lover who has kept me warm is hot, very bright; I will jump into the water, and surrender to its outstretched arms.

There I will feel no pain, no harm and you Gregoriana, my only friend can watch me . . . in case something happens . . . Yes I will jump into the water.

The sky is fuchsia—blue, reflection of sunset in the sky, I used to love it, I have seen it so many times, dreamed so many times, prayed you God . . . so many times.

God have mercy on me, remember my beloved children and you Gregoriana do not forget the promise . . . watch over them.

I cannot anymore, I'm gone, liberated. I have become one being with the infinite sea itself. I am part of this huge universe.

The Footman has hold of my arm and smiles at me.

That awful smile. that I have dreaded for so long, now is natural.

God will not forgive me . . . I cannot stop to think. The water pulls me down to the bottom and I have lost my senses, but gained in spiritual freedom I am beyond my limits of pain and despair in relief and peace . . . God save my soul. Amen

The sun is high in the sky and I feel its kiss upon my forehead . . . slowly I wake up to a new day.

My sheet is soaked wet, I am extremely tired. Gradually, I realize I had a bad dream but I cannot remember anything about it.

I only know that I feel brand new and eager to go out there and kiss everyone I meet . . .

Thank God I am here to enjoy the gift he has given me . . . I would have the courage to open it. If only I knew how!

One year has gone by since I began to open my heart to you. A dull, sullen year.

My two sons have moved away for good. I have refused the job I had been chasing all my life. Is it so important? So many times, I have set my trust in something that after a while has vanished leaving me with a taste of bitterness, hard to get rid of . . . decisions that time will reverse at a wink of the eye. My place is here where dying begins, no hesitation, no diversion.

OLD FRIENDS

Such a sad evening was unexpected.

The sky grew greyer and greyer, heavy with rain, and it dropped like a hammer on the back of my painful neck . . . the humidity in the air . . . a tight rope running loose around it. My hands to my face hide from my sight the boats gathered around and below sunbathing without any sun awaiting for a miracle . . . my guests are due in a while.

Everything is ready, I am not in the mood for fancy parties anymore . . . getting old.

My friends are from my childhood. They come from where my derelict roots still lay in some forgotten corner of this world.

I wonder if I will bore them or they will annoy me. I only get to be around foreigners, no one that has known me. when I lingered in the arms of innocence and thought that fairy tales were real, expecting to grow up and chose the loveliest one . . .

As soon as they enter the gate, fifty years are thrown over my shoulders, dear friends from long ago and from far away.

One memory brings along other stories of when we were young.

There is some relief in all this . . . The notion that I had been free once occurs to my mind and makes my heavy burden lighter to carry . . . I could picture myself as a, chubby, happy child laughing away while skipping down the road, or later shy teenager full of fanciful dreams that have never come true.

I could revive the warm joy of those days when everything was fresh and still to be revealed.

The world was out there at hand, all I had to do was grab it. I could not go wrong . . .

Then he left, my father, leaving me totally unprepared . . . how could I have any knowledge of death at the age of twenty? He had brought me here from far away and then parted, leaving me with an empty heart and very few dreams to hold on to.

But this night has brought me back to the time when all this had yet to be.

Time has gone, past is past. I will retire for the night.

Suddenly, I am caught in the trap of my own rage.

My mind is pervaded by anger directed to what I missed or have no longer. Anger for the end of this ride without return, for things I haven't done or the ones I regret having accomplished.

I hate myself and the emptiness within.

One day I will take revenge of all this: disillusion. Will you, really? Yes of course . . . cool off, please.

Right now the moon inspires calm and acceptance. Goodnight, please.

STEFANO AND LOVE

My mobile phone rang and there was nobody on the other side: silence and cold expectation. These calls had often occurred and I began to worry, being alone in the house, Greg, my dear tower, was sound asleep,

The harbor bay winkled at me from behind her magnificent back. The moon reflected its mysterious light upon the coast and every creature was gone, swallowed by the dark. At a distance someone was singing a song.

The day had been unbearably hot. Now that the wind was blowing softly, people could relax at last and enjoy the breeze.

The owl on the mountain kept making its creepy noise and all I could do was sit still and wait. I had no knowledge of what I was waiting for but I felt that I could not go to bed.

The hours slipped by and at last I perceived a light coming from the sea. I could see the shadow of a boat, red and yellow lights flashing in the dark. It was silent in movement, slow and steady. I could not see anyone on the vessel as it moved along and came closer.

As the vision approached further, my sight was blurred, up to the point that I almost fainted and whatever was there disappeared. Suddenly I felt very tired and retired for the night, aware that more had yet to come.

The following day, no sign of any odd detail.

I ran to the rocks down below, leaned against the rail as much as I could looking for clues in the strange visit, all for naught.

Days went by and I forgot the strange vision, caught in the net of survival.

One afternoon as I sat on my chaise lounge trying to find some relief from the heat, I perceived a presence at the same time real and fantastic. An old man with a long white beard and a sarcastic smile seemed to be leaning over me.

I sat up at once as fast as I could. I had heard the description of him so many times from the people in town, so immediately I knew it was Stefano.

He stood right in front of me; average in height, made shorter and emaciated by age and hardships, long curly white hair. Had they ever been combed?

His white beard had been exposed to time and sun, in years and years of sun and sea.

His patched cloak was a mix of grey, brownish black with dark red stains. Blood?

His eyes, I could not escape those eyes . . . He stared at me searching that soul of mine deep, deep somewhere inside; blue eyes made of the water down below and the sky up above.

He had watched over the bay all his life, until he disappeared . . .

He had been the guardian of the tower long before I was around.

Born in Naples, in one of its many deprived neighborhoods, where neither sun nor air ever gets through, he sucked poverty with maternal milk. Left on the streets alone by an uncaring mother, he struggled to survive. Hardships and humiliations were his only companions and instructors.

Eighteen, he was only eighteen, an old child of the street of his city when he was sent to fight in World War I. He had been fighting for his life ever since he could remember. On the border canons echoed throughout the valley. Death and destruction were scattered on the ground for miles, as far as the eye could see.

But Stefano had been trained by life to be fearless as it made no sense to be overtaken by emotion.

The worst thing that could happen would be death for most but not for him. Death would have brought peace at last to a tormented child, the end of violence that had nourished his body and battered his soul.

So he fought the war, chased by the Footman on the battlefield, without a clear notion of what was going on or what he was doing there . . .

It often happens that we go throw hardships and sorrowful events that shock our imagination, and we don't even realize the courage and endurance it took to get through.

He had been courageous and fearless but confusion was all he could feel.

So when it was over Stefano, like many others, stumbling over what were once bodies, tried to find his way "home." Although he had no place to go, he instinctively headed south towards Naples.

TERRACINA AND DONNA OYMPIA

But a strange thing happened while he was sitting on the train. Disgusted by the reek of dried blood and shit on himself and the other passengers, he suddenly felt nausea from deep inside. It was not the smell in itself but perhaps the memories of the war it brought to him or the anguish of uncertainty in the return to the place of his childhood and a hopeless tomorrow.

Returning to Naples had no meaning and was frightful. In a flash of memory it was reliving his life as he had always known it and it was frightening.

He did not want to go back. He was fed up with pain and sorrow, so he got off the train at the first station. The sign read: Terracina. He landed on the street corner, a forgotten, ragged bundle hardly human anymore. At the same time, Donna Olympia got off the train in her off-white summer outfit, first class wagon, coming from Rome. Her wide brim, demur looking hat, caressed her rosy cheeks, protecting her from the harsh rays of the sun. Her servant, grumpy old lady, followed carrying huge suitcases that were to treasure her mistress' summer wardrobe. Certainly guests would be coming to the villa and she would not, in any circumstance, wear the same dress twice. No war would bring her to give up her refined elegance. It had slightly brought a change, but certainly up to the point of having to give up such priorities!

She, the owner of Torre Gregoriana, was to stand out as always and possible even more so this year.

Her beauty had always been praised by whoever came near but also her elegance and her refined manners were a matter of admiration.

It was by chance she passed by Stefano sitting at the corner of the street, begging in out stretched hands for anything she was willing to give with his eyes empty as his stomach.

She looked at him carefully, perceiving a man who carried the wounds of indescribable suffering in his eye.

She stared with her deep blue eyes into his, plunging down deep into his soul and saw what there was to see.

Donna Olympia bent down closer to that bundle of rags not at all frightened by his appearance, and with a soft, gentle voice asked him to follow her.

She had decided to take him home, feed him, give him new clothes and shelter him for a while.

The sensitive lady had spotted in those eyes, undefeated honesty and pain she could not bear to see unattended.

Once they reached Torre Gregoriana his heart skipped a beat. He had never seen anything so beautiful. The tower, built on top of a rock, stretched out on the bay. The fortification was surrounded by the clear, blue sea and the blue sky above it. Palm trees in the garden offered shade from the unbearable summer heat while purple Bougainville and blue plumbago stood joyful expectation.

The scent of the sea and the vegetation gradually filled his nostrils while the smell of his clothes and the nausea it caused subsided along with any thought of pain and suffering. Joy in the waves, in the flowers and in the lady's smile spoke of contentment. He was alive again and he loved it. The tower was magnificent and protective, just like Donna Olympia and he fell in love with both.

The summer went by as in a dream. Stefano little by little regained his strength. He was a handsome young man who wore the scars of hardship upon his face with pride and wisdom.

He helped out around the house with chores too heavy for the housekeeper. He was useful, clever and everyone in the house liked him.

THE GUARDIAN OF THE TOWER

Autumn approached. It was time for Donna Olympia and her little court to leave.

She had watched Stefano throughout the weeks and knew she could trust him. She never asked him about his family but instinctively she knew there was none.

A week before leaving she decided that Stefano should be the guardian of the tower in her absence; the guardian of the tower as in ancient times, that is. He would stay and look after the needs of the tower; repair damages caused by frequent storms, clean the garden and keep the house orderly.

The padrona offered a small salary, enough for food and fuel and he willingly accepted it.

Days became years in the passage of time. It was always the same, yet different as each day renewed itself in a show of sorts. The clouds drew marvelously diverse and unique paintings in the sky.

The waves, moving in concert played music, sometimes softer and sometimes harder to the ear.

The wind added to the sky show that had as its focal point the sun. It would appear in the morning with diverse shades of red to pink and from time to time shaded by colors of grey, in a rare spot of black.

Peace and beauty surrounded Stefano and he couldn't get enough of it. On most days he sat outdoors after his evening meal and watched the returning fishermen in their boats full of the day's catch. He heard their voices in song as they approached the harbor. The sound brought to mind a distant time, perhaps a memory in song as a child. He wasn't sure.

The breeze under the shade of the palm tree was heavenly and he thought it to be paradise on earth. Winters were short but fierce. He stayed indoors and would only venture out to do necessary chores or shop for food. He was use to solitude in a life spent alone. In this place he had the birds, the sun and the moon to talk to. He didn't mind being alone at all. There was peace and beauty to soothe and satisfy what his aching heart needed.

With Spring's arrival it was time for Stefano to get started on extra cleaning and pruning. As summer approached Donna Olympia's sand box garden on the main terrace had to be filled.

She had a large area filled with sand and scattered sea shells from the shore below. Stefano lovingly embellished the space with rocks and shrubs carefully arranged for her to enjoy. He spent several days preparing the "beach" garden for his Padrona, one she loved and he made special for her every year.

She stole his heart at first glance and he dedicated his life to her happiness. He promised to watch over her beloved tower and would do so for as long as he lived. He watched her enjoy the sun and smile at the moon, happy as only a child would be. Sometimes her eyes would catch his. In those moments he sensed an affection and deep appreciation of all that he did. Life had not been so kind to her. Her wealthy husband, distant and mean didn't know she was alive. She was alone in a loneliness known and shared by Stefano.

As the years went by her blonde hair began to fade as her dark, tan complexion started to hide wrinkles around her eyes. Life left some scars on her but she seemed to wear them proudly or ignored them. Stefano often wondered. She would always be beautiful in his eyes, the most beautiful creature he had ever seen and he loved her dearly. She felt safe from life's disappointments in his presence, a source of respect and devotion that made her happy.

Sometimes they sat apart from one another on the terrace, she near the "beach" like garden and he on a chair in a corner. But their souls were near, nearer than many others and they were contented.

Stefano's hair was turning a bit grey but his heart was as young as ever. He would watch her from a distance . . . knowing that she would soon go away and he would spend the rest of the year waiting for her return.

DREAMS ARE GONE

Fall came and went, spring arrived but summer did not bring Donna Olympia that year. She died and left him sad and alone.

The maid brought a letter from her addressed to Stefano. In it she asked him to stay on as the guardian of her beloved tower, their companion for so long.

Years passed by and World War II came to be. Stefano, nearly blind engaged a boy from the other side of town to come and read the daily news to him.

Stories abounded on the salvation/damnation by of the American liberators in Naples. He had made a choice to stay away from the city but his soul was tied to it in a mix of hate and love.

His flesh and bones were made of the sea breeze in Santa Lucia and the dirt of via Toledo.

He knew he belonged there as he belonged to Torre Gregoriana, in a destiny like an up-rooted tree sinking to the bottom. And he felt deep in the bottom of his guts that Naples could lose the war but they would never be defeated in spirit.

So he sat as an old man with no tomorrow. Was there any hope of any kind, he wondered as history tends to repeat itself. He fought a war and was living through another, yet he was no hero.

Heroes are handsome, fearless and strong. He was only skin and bones. He never gave a thought to the courage it took to live his life past and present. He dwelt and was ready to die in a ruined house, that he couldn't call his own. The wind blew through broken windows leaving him cold and lost. It was inside and out, nothing but the wind and the sea. Where is God? History gives deceptive illusions.

Stefano was present when the Germans arrived at Torre Gregoriana to establish their headquarters.

They found him in an empty room sitting on an old straw chair near the window with thoughts as his only companion. He was weak. His eyes, devoid of any life, convinced the Germans that he was a harmless old man so they let him alone.

He was part of the scenery like the seagulls, the sparse vegetation and the sea itself and stood in the background, almost invisible, yet helpful. He didn't say a word. They spoke a different language, so why try and communicate?

He spent most of the day on the rocks below putting distance between him, the war and those above.

The days went by slowly, as the place seemed out of time and space.

THE COLLAPSE OF THE GIANTS

The war continued for months until its final dramatic chapter when the Americans moving from Naples advanced towards Rome and further north as liberators while the Germans began their retreat.

The orders were to leave the tower and to move north. Before leaving, they were instructed to mine the place in order to make it harder for the enemy advancing from south, marching to liberate Rome. They set dynamite on the first floor and put the candelas between two stones that once held a stucco ornament. Prior to igniting the explosives, they went to Stefano warning him that the place was about to explode. He did not seem to listen or want to understand.

They repeated the message over and over in broken Italian, certainly enough to be understood.

Stefano turned his head, gazed at them in blue eyes wide open. A tear rolled down his cheek as he thought of the tower's demise and the end of his life as it had been.

He refused to move and why should he? Death meant very little to him.

He came up from the rock, walked towards the tower, looked for his old chair and sat near the window.

The moon was shining upon the water and serenity surrounded him. He was secure with the sea, his only friend and it would not abandon him. It went on singing his song of liberation from pain and need.

The Germans forgot all about him leaving him to his destiny. So many people had been killed during that nightmare called war, what difference could his death make?

They lit the explosives and ran away. It took only a few seconds for the spark to reach the dynamite.

The explosion could be heard kilometers from there.

The aftermath in destruction held up the advancing Americans for a few days.

Some troops headed towards the mountains, while others cleared the way for the tanks to come through. It was the month of May 1944

LOVE AND DEVOTION FOREVER

Stefano's body was never found. Neighbors swear he never left, loyal to the tower and his Padrona to the end. Sometimes when evening brings its shade and sunlight comes to an end, I catch a glimpse of eternity where Stefano surely lives. He is on the rocks, along the path that leads to the tower, sitting at the window staring at the full moon, safe at last. The mighty waves sing to him along with the seagulls "viva Stefano" or whoever he is! "Viva" to all those who live and die for a noble cause, certainly not I.

THE TRAP

Sitting here right in front of the sea, on an early July morning, I can see nothing but foggy light blue, the sky is unclear, the sea is transparent water and my soul is divided by two contrasting principles clearness and confusion . . . they have always been my mates; nothing is as it "clearly" seems. It is like jumping off a cliff into the water with your eyes wide shut . . . life I mean . . . you really cannot predict what will really happen.

The weekend is over, hopefully never to repeat itself . . . Greg we are getting too old for parties. The procession with its lights was on as usual and the bunch of people I invited all showed up. But the thrill has gone . . . I cannot pretend something that is not . . . I have changed or perhaps I only see things differently from a year ago. Nothing ever remains the same although nothing really changes. Stefano knew all that long ago.

God must be somewhere nearby I am aware of this, perhaps I will find Him. My life has been a failure. I was brought up a creature without a will, no defense and here I am now.

I "live" this life as in a trap playing the part of the mouse.

I cannot run away. Life has me by my tail and I hang there as its pawn knowing that when it is over there will be no mercy for me. I am afraid to live here, to wake up and wonder what the day will bring.

At night I wake up in fear, a pure unadulterated fear that overcomes me. My mind refuses to accept these thoughts because it is "nonsense", yet they are here.

There is no one to run to, except God, me of little faith. I am not spiritual in thoughts or actions which could nourish my soul, rather shallow when it comes to my existence.

"You are there when I need you. You come shining through and are always there for me."

Those are the words of the song playing on the radio right now, miracle or coincidence. Loneliness; the days pass by in loneliness interrupted only by violence.

Words become swords prepared to stab without mercy, threatening silence in a calm liken to waves before a bursting storm.

THE CURSE OF FAIRYLAND

The sea; my mind crosses the sea and goes back to where I lived for a while, far from here in the land of fairies I thought would love me. The sky so blue, you can picture joyful angels playing on the many clouds that transform constantly into different shapes as you look at them. The sea wild and free has no boundaries and no refrain . . . yet sometimes it's as gentle as a caring mother with is new born baby.

Rainbows . . . A world of rainbows. One afternoon, as I was coming home from my stressful job I saw two rainbows in the sky up at the same time . . . everything seemed a dream come true But you cannot trust that place it is instable, changeable, unreliable, wild just like its nature.

You would picture the elves and fairies as loving creatures, so delicate and perceptive. Well there was none of all that. I was a foreigner and they would not accept me. Many foreigners make Ireland their home but they are "blow in" and staying amongst each other

I had dared to move into a conservative Irish neighborhood. Irish stew and pochin. I had entered their secret world; people as friendly and helpful as you would be with a stranger and I was a stranger, certainly the first in that place.

But notwithstanding the kindness of the people, I knew the fairies' curse upon me was fierce and undeniable. I had lost the protection of the goddess of the land. I could feel it in the air and in everything I did.

Maura, the dead old mistress who, still "lived "in the house I had bought, did not accept a foreigner in her place just as much as I could not accept it myself.

Tiny lady with her glasses set upon her nose dissected me in a glaze from the picture on the wall and decided I had to leave.

I had made that long journey to that land, along those shores so distant from here to find a place to rest my weathered being. But no way . . . I was wrong.

Soon will be the winter solstice. My mind goes back to Dromberg, West Cork, the Druids and their excitement on that day; sun beams on their altar . . . never even near . . . illusion, uncertainty, dreams fables . . . I was not welcome; I had to leave not knowing what to do.

A NEW ILLUSION

Greg has greeted me here, yet I am not safe . . . .
I do not belong here.

I have no roots, or no roots I can count on. I tend
to stick to a place or to people for this reason and this
makes things worse, for me of course.

The universe keeps moving on, no importance, but
it is important to me, has always been.

There was a mistress in this place just before me:
Elisabeth. I often think of her and fear she might not
want me here.

I am like a stray dog, chased from everywhere I
go. Please let me stay. I am the Guardian of the Tower,
am I not?

Am I powerful or vulnerable? Who can tell?

The wind blows and I can almost hear the voice of
Elisabeth and her son arguing across the waves.

She was a foreigner, beautiful and brave but
selfish. Her books, too many drinks, little time for the
children she happened to have delivered during an
unhappy marriage.

When she passed away she was two years older
than what I am now . . . Greg you were there and did
not help.

Will you help me, you selfish pile of sand and stones without a heart . . . you will let me go as you did with all the others Olympia, Stefano, Elisabeth, the Moor in the painting.

I cannot rely on you at all. I thought you were my friend . . . confusion, blurred sight and dizziness . . . need my happiness pills.

THE REAL THING

The morning has put an end to my tormented, induced sleep.

I cannot see anything coming along that could change the greyness of this awakening. Yet the image of a child I saw on the beach keeps rolling in my mind . . . She could have been five or six and was selling picture frames; a few dangling in her tiny hands, small colorful kitsch pieces of incomprehensible art she sold as frames: only for a few cents, colorful pieces of happiness.

She was very serious about what she was doing; no playing on the beach but walking and walking under the sun to make a little money that she could certainly not keep for her.

She had a sad, ancient look in her eyes as if she had understood and accepted the ruthless rules of life. There was firm acknowledgement; life is not a game, it is serious and you just should not fool around with it.

I asked her which frame would she pick and she selected the fanciest, most colourful one.

The girl in the frame was a blonde happy looking child possibly her same age; what she would have liked to be, So with a sigh she handed it out to me and

I gave her what she asked for and a little extra, hoping she would get an ice cream with that . . . shame on me for being so snob and hysterical!

Greg, I am stating that none of the things I had planned for this final stage of my life has turned out to be what I had planned when I first started, none.

Some are worse; perhaps some are better but just not like I had planned.

In some cases they have actually materialized as I expected but did not have the impact they were supposed to have.

Greg, I mean that I had dreamt of spending the rest of my life as your guardian, alone on this solitary rock right in middle of nowhere . . . the lady of mercy for all, the consolatory.

Sitting on a rock watching the tide roll in and out, awaiting for the pirates that are far from here and will never come.

Sterile objectives, empty life . . . to guard a ruin on top of the sea.

Furthermore I must be careful; I cannot stay here alone, as you may know by now.

Soon I will be leaving, yes leaving again aware of the urge deep inside, no purpose in staying.

You do not need me, just like everyone else I love.

You certainly do not need a guardian; you are sovereign of this place, the eternal goddess of the rock and the bay.

We are just passersby and will not stay and you know that. Just like Maura you want me to go and I will obey, no use opposing resistance.

You decide of my destiny, you are the devil burning inside. Please let me stay. I am too tired to move on.

I shall stay one way or the other.

The boys came last night; my body and soul immediately got back to life.

If only my eldest would stay just for a few days . . . I do not reckon that there will be any other chance for being together like this . . .

A FAILED FARWELL

I remember, it was many years ago, yet it is as if time stopped then and there. She, my mother laws dying in an hospital bed.

The TV was on and she asked me with a solemn yet imploring voice to lay next to her as we had done so many times before and watch the programmed together . . . I knew that would have been the last time and I recalled at once all the times as a child and even much later what it meant to me laying next to her.

As a child, assaulted by fear of the mysterious darkness, I would run to her warm side. When disappointed by any event life would bring I would find comfort and safety in her arms.

Then lying on that hospital bed, would have been a sort of magic, religious farewell. An initiation to adulthood. Gone was any sort of comfort from fear and disillusion. Any generous distribution of love would have disappeared at once from my life, forever. I knew I had to grab the chance and lay there.

But while I was moving towards the bed, the doctor came in and all these opportunities vanished in the air

Gone. She left and I still regret that missed opportunity. That night I sat next to her bed. I had taken some pills and I was in a foggy state of mind.

Darkness had stretched its wings along the obscure corridors of the hospital and wrapped it up in appalling silence; not a stir, a whisper, a sound. Time had stepped aside to allow eternity to enter the place. The wind began to blow soft and silent through the uncertain windows.

Time without end there; infinite and yet contained in the small room where my mother laid dying and I, helpless creature, distant spectator of a miracle.

The angel of death raised its pitiful arm and enveloped the poor aching body on the bed. I felt a soft blow behind my neck and she was gone.

I stood confused, startling at the event of death, so mysterious yet so real and natural. One quick blow and life is gone. Incredible. pain, sorrow, hopes, joys and expectations, achievements and failures disappear in one soft blow, like a candle in the wind.

Son please stay. I know it is nonsense, if I ask you to stay. I even know that you will refuse, but please stay, give a few moments of your life to me before we part . . . each of us following our own path.

You hopefully will ride the clouds of glory and fame. My path is clear enough . . .

The Guardian of the Tower

I am boring, hysterical but please stay. I am so alone; my soul is deep empty, pitch bottomless . . .

You have all your life . . . . I wish you all the best, but now please don't go.

WHERE ARE YOU CHRISTMAS?

He has gone. They are all gone and the waves down below keep roaring and banging against the walls, against my heart. My head keeps pounding hard and I hope my happiness drops will be enough to bring me back.

Santa Claus is coming to town . . . . where are you Christmas?

The tree is decorated. The lights are up. Music pervades the empty rooms . . .

I sit on the chair sip my coffee; change my chair since nothing else ever changes.

I've decorated so many Christmas trees in so many different places, aware that it would be the last Christmas there . . . actually I have hardly ever spent two Christmases in a row in the same place.

This is my first time here with you Greg. Christmas just the two of us . . . alone.

Two of my three children will be coming . . . a few days and then gone again.

I've added pain to pain like pulling out three teeth at one time. You get tired . . . of this dreadful game of Fate . . . I am no hero.

I'd rather gives up my motherhood, for what it is worth, forget all about them . . .

But then they call for advice, I make an effort to return to my maternal role, enter into their soul and try to understand what their problem is and try to help . . . But this is what keeps me alive . . . I live only in those few moments, it is unexpected.

Perhaps another year has gone by now. It seems like ages . . .

You Turkish Moor on the ceiling, were you alone in this world?

Was your loss a pain for someone . . . or was your existence and disappearance ignored.

Life worth a dime?

Wars fought conquered and lost, men come and go. My boys are caught in the modern struggle to survive and live a decent life. They must go.

Mothers are cheated from the beginning; once you are pregnant there is no morally acceptable escape.

No purpose in friends, parties, social life . . . wearing a mask of fake smiles and false comments . . . pretending I am not alone.

The sea, the sun are my friends not more distant then the rest. I can feel their warm embrace.

At night, the sea sings to me a lullaby without a name, Stefano knows how sweet it could be, how reassuring; like being in the arms of a strong, courageous lover that would challenge the monsters of your soul to keep you alive and smiling . . .

The sun peeps throw the shutters to smile at me, the only smile I will see the whole day but usually it is enough to give me a reason to live . . .

God is there, I know, somewhere but I keep losing track of him and the rest of the group . . . it gets harder and harder to pray as the days go by . . . no sense in my existence, no reason for it.

As soon as I awake and perceive the glimpse of life I begin to shiver . . .

New Years tonight. My two boys here with me and my husband, prisoners of our selfish love.

Nothing to say no real interaction, fake curiosity, fake answers.

During the holidays I have taken pictures of everything that happened, even the most insignificant to keep all this for eternity.

But what is it that I am trying to retain, something that has disappeared long ago, long before I had realized it . . . it is all over.

In its place illusions of motherhood . . .

I should have gone on with my own life, if I had knew what it was like and let them go and grow without a feeling of guilt that I reckon I must have nourished.

This morning, like every morning, I wake up with the anguish that never subsides but that in the silence of my room amplifies, expands, fills three small rooms until I need to breathe and rush out for air.

Anguish made up not of irrational thoughts or feelings of a perverse mind, but of the clear, sharp awareness of the passing of time and of my impossibility neither to stop nor to live. It has passed me by and has left me unaware . . .

I wake up because I am afraid of my empty self incapable of appreciating existence for what it is; a cloud, an inconsistent entity that holds together small events joys and sorrows, birds, trees, mountain and seas, love, hatred, despair and fulfillment.

I am just incapable of jumping in, so I watch the cloud pass by with its pink and blue tint and sit aside in the dark, frightened, waiting, and inactive for my time to come.

BUSINESS

On the main square of this town, I am trying to call my own, many branches of small ancient alleys rush like rivulets towards the sea.

Small, simple houses that once were huts stand on the edge of the road, like friendly faces where the sun shines and you feel alive.

One day an old lady was sitting on the doorstep of one of these cottages, selling tasty plum tomatoes from her garden. She was a peasant used to hard work. But now she was too old and ill.

The day was hot, as usual on a summer day but I had overcome my laziness and with my son I just happened to pass by.

I saw the tomatoes and was very happy to buy the whole bunch from her . . . but to my surprise this made her sad . . . she started to cry saying she wouldn't have anything else to do for the rest of the day now that she had sold her patch of vegetables. I can see what she meant now.

Emptiness that nothing can fill, life that is going by and you are still too active to let it go . . . it is a struggle and you know you must give up.

The silence of the day continues into the silence of the night and carries my soul away into a world out of this world where nothing is possible, where everything is still, unmovable, death before death, I can hardly breathe, in the stillness of it all.

The waves move according to an eternal, steady rhythm, always the same, day after day, night after night, no change. This apparent death that brings to death . . . no difference? There must be, but I cannot see it. If I could find it I would be saved . . . help me see the difference . . . .

THE BOY WITH A DREAM IN THE PROMISED LAND

The coal mines are shut down; the steel mills are silent, now.

People have lost in their dreams. But the US used to be the promised land where dreams could come true.

He was only 17 in 1905 . . . 40 dollars in his pocket and adventure in his grey blue eyes when he sought the dreams that had nourished his soul.

The village on the mountains suffocated his ambition and left him no space to breathe. So he got his part of heritage, after his father had passed away and left.

He had had enough of his sobbing mom and three younger brothers to worry about. There must have been something for him somewhere, and somehow he would find it.

The ship was there, at the pier:

Italia, its name sounded majestic and a bit nationalistic, too patriotic for someone like him who was leaving his native land that offered no hope no fulfillment of dreams.

His grey eyes looked up at the huge vessel and rested on its belly, where he would be confined with scarcely any food and little air to breathe for a month. But it was worth it.

Once there, in the promised land, he would be reborn to life, a real life for the first time.

Many like him had their pockets full of dreams and their stomachs empty.

The days went by quickly. If there is hope for a young 17 year old, the adventure confounds itself with reality.

Ambition, dreams are real, at that age and he was going after them no matter what.

He had left behind his sad mom and nagging brothers, free at last to conquer the world starting from the city that spreads its wings over the ocean.

It was huge but he would find his way. Couldn't bother with people stared at him, labeling him.

It wasn't easy to get off the ship, papers were to be filled, and information, questions he could hardly understand.

His cousin was waiting for him and he was anxious to get off. Happiness in a new life was waiting for him in out stretched hands.

At last they let him go and him.

He started running, running and running on legs that needed to feel solid ground after the precarious steadiness of the ship on the ocean. He started shouting, words without a meaning just to hear his voice and make sure it was all real. His heart began to pound hard as he ran towards his cousin's place.

The streets were dingy and dirty but what could you expect?

He was not looking for a castle but for a chance, only a chance for freedom and happiness that derives from fulfillment and safety.

His cousin was a short man with long with grey moustache, not talkative but kind. He offered him a small, dark space, which used to store potatoes for good money. In the dark room the 17 year old with a heart full of dreams got a bed but couldn't fall asleep for the excitement.

The day after he would start digging, he was told that digging would have been his future for as long as he wanted. He decided to give it a try.

He was strong, not much muscles on the guy with still one foot into childhood. But he would have built his muscles along the way.

Three years, three years went by, digging and building up his muscles. But he forgot his dreams under the weight of all the hard work and stale beer.

He had enough of digging. Home, was better after all. So he went to the ticket office and bought a ticket. He wanted to go back, never to leave again.

Life has its ways that nobody can understand. So that forgotten man, no longer a boy is buried in a forgotten cemetery in a forgotten place, far from his country not far from the coal mines where he used to dig as a young boy.

He could not decide of his destiny, no matter what.

The reason he was there is another story . . . too long to tell.

I heard about this unlucky guy from my friend who had known someone who had meet someone else who had heard his story.

But I am not leaving, not looking for new adventures, I am here to stay. I am to protect Greg and she is to protect me for as long as I live.

No more dreams will make me move from this place I have just started to call home.

The music from the radio (smooth jazz) tells me that there is nothing out there for me anymore. There has hardly ever been.

I have been blessed with this place and I should stay as long as the Footman, leaning against the wall and staring at me, will let me. That is more than enough. The waves crash against the rocks and the whole house seems to tremble.

GLORY DAYS IN PRAGUE

Empty silence fills the room; words unspoken or too often repeated like swords, as a new day shuffles in heedless of what is to come.

All of a sudden I look outside and I perceive a light so clear, pure. It is a heavenly light that seems to promise wonders . . . I have been deceived so many times that I just cannot absorb and take in the emotion anymore.

Yet I have to believe in something and this is what I have.

I will put on a smile, stand up open the door and go for a walk . . . or should I stay and do some gardening.

On the main street people will say ". . . she is getting old, look at her grey hair, her outfit out of fashion, so ordinary . . . She has changed so much since she got back from Prague".

Yes, that enchanting city is always dear to my heart. The river Vltava slowly gliding along carries your worries away, while the sun, bright over the numerous ever changing colors of the Baroque/Art Nouveau buildings, opens your heart to another gorgeous day. Prague is beautiful even with the cold freezing weather.

The beauty of the enchanting city seems to warm your heart while the white snow covers the streets, the roofs, the trees and the unreal world becomes magic with a further promise of Beauty.

It is as beautiful as its girls. Happy, smiling girls, conscious of their undeniable, irresistible beauty. It is their awareness that makes them shine as they walk down the boulevard, knowing they are lovely. They look perfect as they sit at the café sipping tea in a cold afternoon or getting on their buses always on time . . . rushing to work. One job is not enough but they are strong and determined to enjoy life, take their chance, work hard to make the money they need to dress up and have a good time.

The spa at the Flora Hotel, modern communist style of the '60 smiled at me, through its glass windows, from beyond the park where everyone was jogging. The spa, soft luxury, exotic music, essential oils in the air, evoked distant places and made me feels a stranger in the place where I was yet a foreigner.

The language barrier was no longer an obstacle as the young girls took care of my aging body. It was the place where I could pamper myself as much as I wanted . . . the girls were all so nice and professional and I would enjoy the caresses that penetrated into the body and the soul. Prague had what I needed to satisfy my craving for art, culture, refined cafés that shone with their gold leaf mirrors.

I could gaze upon my reflection, as I watched people scrutinizing me; there was admiration in their eyes, I knew I was shining and I was pleased.

It had taken me a lifetime to get to that point of self esteem and I enjoyed their glances not at all afraid of their judgment. I was tall and slim, very elegant in my black leather outfit, silver jewels underlining my silver highlighted hair, lovely make up to match, beautiful clothes and a lot of money . . . funny how wealth helps gain confidence . . . materialistic, but it works.

I would buy new outfits for all the parties in town, I was invited everywhere and enjoyed the popularity. I loved being amongst people, interacting with them, gossiping a little. Always smiling, looking beautiful . . . like the girls of Prague?

But it is all over now and . . . nothing will change until the Eternal Footman will put it all to an end . . . . Believe me, girls, it is the boredom that makes the difference and the lack of money.

So why should I go out. Everything is so dull that it makes me lazy, yes that is the word, and I have lost my energy and do not see why I should bother to recover it. Lost.

FREEDOM AND AWARENESS

The day went on in an up and down attitude whether to go out or not, until my spirit got dizzy and put itself to sleep. The chaise long was there and my will was not.

So I dreamt of a place where everything would be as it used to be. But this time I would take it all in, enjoy every moment of what had been given to me.

Three children who looked up to me for help, for advice, for teaching, Yes, I dreamt of my little place out in the country, those shouting voices from yonder. My son Pierangelo coming back with his friends and his shoes covered with mud. I should have enjoyed his youth discovering the world and others instead of yelling at him" Your shoes are dirty can't you see? I've just cleaned up": harsh and selfish. No thought or time for others or for my own self.

You cannot help me, sun, no matter how fiercely you shine. There is no return to the past to those joys ignored, in the desperate search of what joy would not bring . . . False Gods.

Now, the darkness of my soul is too thick for you to penetrate. Under the glitter of your rays upon the water, I see restlessness and another storm.

When my son called the other day, I was pitch blue and thought that nothing could help.

Instead slowly and gradually as his words poured into my aching soul, I began to feel relieved of the pain, as I followed the line of his projects and felt the warmth of his vigorous energy; the power of youth and hope.

I was alive again . . . if only he called more often.

The wind was blowing and the branches of the tree seemed to sing a song. For a fraction of eternity I realized that all this would pass too and never return again. I should grab it . . . but how?

I am living in that future that my intuition allowed me to perceive long ago. There is no coming back to when I was young and beautiful and I had my marvelous children who trusted and believing in a worthless me. It was wonderful. but still there are moments to enjoy, if only I knew . . .

Instead, the night came as a haunted wild bear. It was a heavy fearful night with nightmares and sad thoughts, as there are many. The past is haunting me; my present is due to how I perceived the days gone by. My many past mistakes will cause me to suffer further in the future, unless I learn to see the positive sides of my present . . . Past and present are in my future and I know it is no good . . . I don't think you can get rid of your past and therefore you have no control over your future. They are bonded together for my ruin.

It is so slippery and I will fail.

The awareness of this reality hits me with its distinct sound deep inside my body . . . this silence screaming for love that no one can hear. My sad eyes and grumpy words frighten who I love away. Someday they will disappear.

THE HAPPINESS TREE

The tree, under which our family united, not always in joy, but yet in love, gathered during the summer has withered, has lost its leaves. We would meet under the branches at lunchtime or just to enjoy the shade.

But, although summer is back, those branches are bent as if without life or purpose; no more young people to shelter and to give relief from the Mediterranean heat. I am like the withering tree . . . no doubt about that. Nothing can be done. Unless I try to see beyond the dark.

One day I was walking home under my umbrella and I noticed that someone else was walking next me. My raincoat was soaked wet and my cap, imported straight for Ireland, with red and green flowers dangling on a side was sad and blue.

But the lady walking next to me didn't seem to mind the rain. She kept walking steady and secure dressed in blue and white. Looking at her made me feel comfortable. Then all of a sudden, while I was thinking of the dinner to prepare and the clothes to get out of the washer, she turned around and what I could see of her, struck my attention; her big green eyes, deep and clear looked straight into mine as she said" you must be happy. There are many reasons for you to be happy"

Now, I could not understand how she knew but she went on and added" you are beautiful, you have a beautiful family . . . everything is fine" Then, having said that, she disappeared and I never saw her again in town or around the place.

Angels wasting their time.

REBELLOUS NEIGHBOR

That same evening, I was waiting for some good music from the radio. It is so hard to find something that soothes your soul when it is aching. Music caresses your mind and your spirit and lifts your heart up to the point that there is no more pain, no more sorrow.

All of a sudden, I heard voices outside my gate. The news had spread as a clash of thunder; my neighbor had killed her husband and was expecting the consequences without a word . . . no regret, no despair.

I rushed across the street and found her empty handed and empty hearted. Her eyes were blank, her skin white with drops of perspiration running down her cheeks. The wind was blowing strong and majestic. It sounded like the voice of God himself, frightful and pitiless: eternal justice. Justice.

You almost wonder if God really knows what this lady in her grey, dull, shapeless dress had gone through all her life. Never a word, never a caress. Loneliness as far as she could remember, physical and spiritual blows, many so many they could not hurt her anymore.

But last night she got up from bed with a rage that only time had built up inside of her and found the physical strength to cut his throat and get it over with.

Nothing can be worse than what she had gone through . . . I could almost perceive a smile on her face. You may think she is a criminal. I believe she is a saint.

The police arrived in their blue and dully fake uniforms, blank faces without any sense of life and its pains.

She stood up, a prisoner to be punished. But this time, for the first time since I've known her she stood with her shoulders straight as if she had gotten rid of a heavy burden and was free at last, free to accept her imprisonment that would have been of relief.

I watched her go, never to see her again . . . a few weeks later, the news spread, she had committed suicide in jail . . . no one there, no consolation . . . what is the sense in rebelling if our Fate is there to decide.

Guardian angel what is your relation with Fate? Perhaps your voice is too weak against the insane shouting of our voices and the pounding hard of our hearts.

THE EXPIRING DATE: SEPHEN DEDALUS AT LUNCH

In our beginning is our end. As we come to this world we begin to die, life is a merchandise with an expiring date, only that it is covered by our blind craving for life, for emotions, passions, success and we never, never stop to read the label until it gets washed away by the waves and our tears. So we cannot read the date but we know that there is one.

Uncertain of when it is, we do not dare take the risk to go for it, life I mean, once we remember that there is an expiring date . . . you never find the courage to go for it, for what your heart mostly craves.

My guest arrived for lunch rather late . . . The table was set in the dining room. The vase with pink roses contrasted beautifully with the invading blue of the sea from outside the window.

The sky was blue grey and my heart had the same hue.

He arrived handsome, smart smile while parking his metallic grey spider Alfa Romeo in our driveway. It was hard to tell which was more attractive and powerful in appearance. The fine-looking gentleman, a well known professional, descended from his top class chariot as a demigod of Beauty would descend from Heaven.

Blissful beauty lingered in his features . . . but some sort of restlessness was clear in his blue eyes.

The world seemed to be waiting for his words. I had seen him before, had admired his talent and his looks but had hardly ever heard him speak: "Are we going to do something about this tower?" Were his words.

I have no reason to argue with anyone who would want to renew Greg's looks; however I did not appreciate his comment.

As the day went by I happened to look in those eyes that tried to evade mine . . . I noticed dissatisfaction in that young, handsome, talented man . . . He was forty three: "If I were younger I would do so many things."

He was starting to feel the grip of age, still distant, but there to grab his arm and pull him down.

He knew there were still things he had not done, chances he had not taken.

Fear had kept him from experiencing everything his heart would have wanted to do. So now he carried on with his art, aware of the opportunities gone by, never to return.

He considers his country as the place which restraints his talent but he is conscious that he will never leave.

His childlike sensitivity and imagination have eventually evolved into a near-obsessive contemplation of Beauty and the mechanics of Art.

Carefully and thoroughly thinking about Beauty and the power of art, he has realized that he can do nothing else but pursue his life of artist, stuck in his ivory tower.

Chances are offered only once by the gods and they are "only for the brave", as they say.

His eyes mirrored perfectly well all his anguish and at the same time his childish irresponsibility; cause of his denied fatherhood. No longer a son, he was unwilling to become a father.

A sweet little dog was there to take the place of a child he could call his own. He will grow old but will never mature and his time consuming frustration is all he has to keep him company.

Such a lovely, lonely soul! Perhaps he has been spoilt by life that seems to promise so much with its charms and cheeky smiles.

He is still seduced by Beauty and Art but has a faint intuition that he might be left empty hearted spending his existence, as a renewed Stephen Deadlus, with the illusion that creating art will help transcend worldly woes.

Why do people fear to take chances? I have made several mistakes and I am responsible for having caused much pain and my guilt tortures me, yet I have tried and I certainly do not regret this.

HOUSES AND HOMES

Yes, Greg you are an old ruin, as our guest says. Let's face it. There has been a time for me to dream and see my dreams vanish in the air, a time to enjoy my place. But houses rise and fall, the spirit of the house I mean.

My dear, as a ruin you will always exist . . . But you need someone that cares for you to "be alive".

It is the interaction that gives life to you . . . just like people. You are alive only when you interact with others.

Houses live and die: there is a time for building and a time for living but there is an end . . . to all this.

All goes into the dark, as the senses get cold and we lose a reason for action. Soul please stops, forget yourself and let oblivion fall upon you, like a decaying house that no one cares for.

So time will come for the wind to blow through the loosen window panes, for the rain to pour through decaying walls and everything is gone.

Birds will build a nest in my bedroom and rats will have a party in my dining room.

I will be careless breeze blowing over this nullity, until some day someone will come around and bring everything back to life.

I did it with you Greg; this is why you are my dear beloved creature. I loved you from the start and I know that in a way you have loved me . . . I spent my days bringing you back to life, enjoying parties under your shade, watching the seagulls swimming in the sun while I lay upside down, looking at the world from un unfamiliar perspective, licking my wounds, not so painful after all.

I hosted many friends who came to visit, each with his world, his story, his Fate.

PEACE BITTER SWEET

I sit and watch the morning sun make this world Paradise. The show is on and nothing can distract my attention. The rays of golden light hurt, and my inner sight is blurred . . . I follow the water sliding away, carrying its crystal pearls.

God, your Beauty, and your Power! I thank you for this life and I weep as it is almost over.

My son will soon go forever and I will not be able to follow him.

He will get fed up with the eternal noise of the waves the everlasting nullity of existence that is so clear here, where there are no distractions to confuse your mind. My son, closed, wrapped, barricaded in himself, no time for smiles. Rude to me at any word, mean to others as to himself, and so helpless. He makes me angry but deep is my understanding for him and his sorrows.

I cannot help loving him ever so much. My pain for him grows as I see him unhappy and alone. He is my son and, although it is not to take for granted, my compassion for him is easier than for others.

I have always forgiven my boys with no second thought. It's not always easy with other people.

But my sons are part of me, the best part. They are the part I am most willing to forgive, to encourage, to set free.

The ruined, spoilt, me can stay . . . need not bother to run around not knowing what to do. I have given up the struggle; a white flag is on my door.

I pray God in this glorious morning to have mercy of those innocent creatures I have injured with my insanity preferring my selfish pride to their well being. Many times the sunshine bright and soothing seems to reassure me that God is merciful and loving and will give my boys courage and will forgive me, my nonsense.

THE LADY IN BLUE AND THE GIRL IN PINK

Unexpectedly spring again . . . another year gone by.

The plants, very few around the fortress, were beginning to show signs of expectation, illusions of vitality where my soul could be closer to the eternity. Should I get out of the place and sit in the garden? The dawn was pleasant and inviting . . . nothing to do no care/ occupation in sight . . . I decided to go down to the rocks.

The sunset that morning was an explosion of crimson and gold on the dark blue water. From a distance I perceived a small boat coming towards me. As soon as it got closer I could see a beautiful lady sitting there in a blue robe: dark hair and pale skin graciously aged . . . She was waving at me inviting me to get on with her. The air was clear and I could see the sun rising from behind her shoulders. Its golden reflection was everywhere around her.

Like a portrait framed in blue and gold, she smiled happily at me and I felt reassured, why not go?

So I decided to plunge into that beauty scene, become part of it.

Peace was everywhere around us.

She spoke not a word but all of a sudden I could read into her soul and I knew everything there was to know about her. The boat kept sliding on the calm golden blue water carpet and at the end it brought me back to my rock. Not a word was spoken but I knew her . . . no need of words. I waved goodbye and never saw her again.

Long ago in the small house on top of the hill, far from here, music lingered in the air.

The beautiful lady in the boat was just a young girl then. Taken ill, in her too warm bed she could distinctly perceive the music coming from down below. It was her dad's birthday and a few friends had gathered to celebrate . . . there was hardly any opportunity for fun, so it was hard for her to lay there; she just couldn't.

Young people are so unpredictable, so full of energy, joie de vivre; illusions that time will cancel. Music had attracted her so she stood up, put on her pink robe and descended the stairs.

Her pink robe and ruby cheeks resembled a bunch of roses, beautiful roses kissed by the sun. It was all he could see and was inebriated by the perfume of the flowers, the perfume of youth and beauty and fell in love.

Love often comes when least expected and she, a gorgeous flower, was not expecting it at the age of fourteen . . . But he was handsome, joyful and kind . . .

so love filled her heart and she felt it swallow inside her soul for the first time.

They met the following day and promised each other eternal love . . . but he went away never to show up again.

Life cheats and deceives you at every corner. So after a quickly arranged marriage with another stranger from afar, she was left alone and the years went by.

The war came along and of the unknown spouse, no sign, not a letter reminding her that far away someone still kept her near to his heart.

Alone, yet strong she accepted her condition, stood half way between expectation and resignation and kept on waiting.

Eighteen years later, no expectations from life, she found her husband again.

In due time her heart bloomed with love again, this time for her baby, that was to be her precious child forever.

She had lost love once and would not give it up again this time. I am that child and she is my Mom.

She lingers in the depth of my soul, has never left nor I want her to. She is my adviser, my companion, my torturer, my victim, my always unsatisfied teacher.

I will never learn, she repeats it to me each day. I have given up the struggle long ago, never actually had the strength to fight back, except with hoarse, insane words, no actions no propositions . . .

Here I am after a boat ride with my mom, yelling at the moon that has just come up.

PERFECTION

Dreams hardly ever come true and if you dream of perfection . . . You are most likely to be disappointed.

I have hardly ever been really forgiven, if there really was anything to forgive. Yet my mom always made me feel terribly responsible for not being perfect.

Greg you should have met my mom, tall and abundant, but of a beautiful kind. Dark hair and a beautiful smile whenever she decided to gift me with her smile. As a child I grew up as her jewel, her precious little toy. I was a baby doll, a puppet she would pull on her string . . . with love, of course yet I was treated as a beautiful, wonderful doll not to let go of, never.

Lovely little creature, with curly hair. Mother would put curlers on it every night because "curly is nice." My hair was not natural curly . . . so something was to be done to correct nature.

I was a lively child always active, too active to gain weight. She liked chubby children, far from the starving poor creatures she had seen during the war in Italy. So I had to eat and eat until I developed a habit for food that caused me trouble during the years.

But I was closer to the image of the perfect daughter she had dreamt of for so long . . . Thirty seven years she had waited for this miracle to happen and now she had a child to model as if out of clay, according to her desire.

In first grade, when I began to learn to write, I would use my left hand. But, a perfect child, the ones you dream of, the heavenly sent, use their right hand, so I had to learn, if I wanted to please her.

I would grab a toy with my left hand and I would see contempt in those eyes that I loved so dearly and my only desire would be to punish myself for having caused her pain.

She was all I had and all I relied on . . . I was nothing without her. I felt that way as the years went by. I was far from being a perfect child, always did the wrong thing, and said the inadequate words in the most inappropriate way and place. I got so angry with myself for not knowing what was the right thing to do and yet she would repeat it to me but, although I concentrated on those mysterious words that spoke of correct behavior, dignified attitude, people's criticism or admiration, I just couldn't get to grip to their meaning and importance.

I was to be the most admired, respected, person in the world. She thought that this would make me happy as an adult, thus carried on her education plan without mercy.

Year after year, I became more and more convinced of the importance of being perfect and how impossible it would be for me to achieve this result.

I was condemned to failure and to cause pain to the only creature I really loved and admired.

Never in my mind had I stopped to consider the possibility that there could be another truth made of calm, relaxation, fun . . . tenderness. I had to cope with anxiety for performance, rush towards something other than what I had. I should please her.

She was too special to have me as I was and I wanted to make her happy and keep her love. If I was unsuccessful in some task, I could perceive her distant contempt and all my efforts had been vain.

At school, of course I was to be the best. The best, these words still pound hard in my head . . . and I failed each time to be the best . . . perhaps close to it, but never the best.

It seemed so important to her and along the years it began to be important to me, just because I have never known anything else. All my life I kept spying with the corner of my eye her reaction to the news of my school or career success, but something always seemed to be missing.

Of course I would react to her with bitterness and harsh words, only to make things worse. My sense of guilt would grow to choke me and I would feel dizzy.

My relationship with others has been shaped on the same line . . . I have always refused to follow any expectations from others fearing to disappoint them. I am convinced that I am inappropriate to anyone's happiness because in the end, I fear I will lose them.

Therefore I need their constant praise and approval . . . that hardly ever comes . . . so far from perfection. So I realize I have failed again, each time I try to love.

Nevertheless I have modeled my boys according to the same horrible line . . . . Perfection.

I am aware now that it cannot be so important but I have no substitute for it . . . . I have become the torturer of myself and my innocent children in this lost pursuit for perfection . . . job, clothes, house everything was and still is supposed to be perfect . . . my impossible rush towards the ultimate ideal for myself and my off springs has caused me pain and gloomy days.

She has gone long ago, so long I cannot remember her face. Only the love I had for her still hurts.

Yes, it is all inside along with the regret for having been unsuccessful in making her happy; I was the only one who could . . .

Now this anger makes me nasty with the ones I love who are innocent victims of irresponsible relations and expectations. Words make things worse, as it is hard to explain the explosive blend of guilt and anger I carry inside. The tenderness I feel right now, because of the early morning sun and its promise, I know perfectly well by now is precarious if not illusory . . . it is like walking on broken glass, on a gelatin bridge that is very likely to collapse.

Three long, dreadful years have gone by since I am here with you and all of a sudden, I can see frightfully clear, that I have not achieved a thing, not even become familiar with my new self and what new purpose is there for me in this limbo.

People think I am cool. Sometimes they have even envied me. I dress up, have parties, lead my apparently pleasant life . . . inside I am poor and starving to death, You know that Greg; you've seen me craving for spiritual nourishment so many times . . .

I would do anything to get rid of this terrible feeling that tortures me. But I choose the hurtful way, hurt the ones I mostly love, chase them away, to punish myself.

I cannot forgive myself. Mercy; there is not such a word in my vocabulary for me or for others. Yet I feel that the secret lies in forgiveness . . .

RECOVERING MEMORIES AND JOY

Despite or because of the continuous disregard of my mother at my attempts to find my way in life, despite the hardships I found along the road, many and difficult to endure, I have always thought Iwould succeed in creating the life I desired for myself and my dear ones.

My ambition would lead me. I would work hard and have it all.

In a way I have always thought my life would be special, perfect, we may say. But here I am, sitting alone in an empty room, watching the waves banging against the windows, tall, enormous, suffocating waves.

Life is teaching me that I have followed a false perspective, perfection, success cannot be the point.

In time I might learn to appreciate what I have, recognize the things I have achieved no matter what, if I am lucky, or I will die desperate and bitter, as nothing will change.

I am tired of fighting against the breeze that exasperates my being, the wind that all confuses and makes what is perfect, imperfect and free. So I go back to my empty silence that stabs like a knife. I look inside myself, in search of something to hold on to but it is a dark and empty room.

Darkness and fear, memories that bring back anguish and regret, an aching heart: silence and turmoil at the same time.

I roam in the depths of my soul searching but there seems to be nothing and I keep falling, and falling into a bottomless pitch.

I am wandering along the narrow alleys of my soul and just around the corner, I perceive a dim light, faint apparition of brightness that cuts the darkness like a blade and recognize indistinctly images of my past, this time made of love: my baby entering this world, feeding at my breast, my first kiss under the sun, my son calling my name, my boys laughter and joy, their expectations . . . their discovery of a new world, beautiful places I have seen, many friends I have made . . . appreciation.

I have forgotten all these and many other treasures . . . memories that belong to the past, never to return again. Bitter sweet truth. They were happiness and perfection themselves.

. The sun shining after a storm, the magnificent view of the stars, my children that still are near at least in their heart, a walk on the shore, shells and colorful shells, others wonderful things happening to me right now, If I learned to look well into depths and listened to the sound of beauty I could enjoy them.

No beauty for me, no happiness. The sun is out but soon it will rain again and I am bored with walking along the shore gathering useless shells. I ignore the good things I have in this moment or take them for granted:

I have seen the light . . . just a glimpse of light then darkness again . . . I must learn to let myself go and forget perfection/ dissatisfaction.

". . . forget all your troubles all your cares . . . come downtown", as the song goes. But there is no "downtown" that can save me from my destructive thoughts, I know that.

I have seen some of the most beautiful downtowns in the world: Naples, Athens, Tunis New York, Paris, London, Dublin, Rome, Madrid, Prague but they are all the same.

This "downtown" must be inside our souls. A place of freedom, joy and love. But I am pitiless, skeptical and cruel in the first place with myself. It is impossible to escape from yourself. You will remain your own prisoner if you don't let yourself go and . . . live for whatever life is worth . . .

MY TORTURERS AND MY ESCAPE

But that old lady with a faded blue and white dress is staring at me from behind her spectacles; her eyes, two round marble balls, play with my spirit. The sun cannot warm her soul.

She keeps telling me what I should, what I should wear, what to do with my life making me feel out of place wherever I go. I don't like any of her suggestions . . . yet I do what she says.

The dark grumbling man stares at me from the corner of his empty eyes . . . not a word is ever spoken, not a smile, no appreciation for whatever I have achieved.

He gives me only bitter remarks for what I should have done, or done better.

No satisfaction in all my life from him. No kindness nor a pat on my shoulder . . . I am alone and miserable. Insanity fills the air.

That old lady keeps staring at me and comes in without notice sits at my table and as I begin to talk, she interrupts me and repeats that I am wrong, always have been.

My projects are only dreams without a future, bound to fail like all the others . . . I sit still and watch the storm arising from the sea and think she is right.

Suddenly I stop dreaming and wait, wait for nothing to happen . . . she smiles with that witchlike smile that hurts deep inside and tells me it is too late . . . I agree.

So she stands up as if she had never sat, and like a walking shadow goes away, leaving my soul devoid of any resource, any strength.

They have taken all my dreams away, torn the essence of my soul apart, made a paper ball of my being kicking it far from me. I am only a shadow of myself.

But I will not let all this destroy me; once you are aware of the tricks of life, of its risks and hardships . . . you learn to accept them . . . and give up.

This can be your only salvation. Renounce to struggle and set yourself free.

"Because I do not hope to turn again because I do not hope in this man's fortune . . . no longer I strive to reach such things . . . Because these wings are no longer wings to fly . . .

. . . Teach us to care and not to care

Teach us to sit still . . ."

T.S.Eliot ASH WEDNESDAY

FORGIVE

I must forgive this fragile, innocent me. I have always looked at myself from the outside. My life has never belonged to me.

Those actions, words, swords, tears, joys were not mine. What was going on was not my choice. I should go back and take full responsibilities for my life and consciously "feel" the pains but also gain awareness and total possession of the joys that have gone with it.

What is left of my life is a short time, but it is and must be only mine. It belongs to me, although I don't know how to handle it. I have not been trained to freedom. I fear I might spoil it . . . . and I probably will.

The wind blows through the doors. the rain pours from the ceiling. The clouds are grey; no answer fills the silence of the empty room of my soul.

When I think back on my life, there are names that will forever make me sad and yet, in every single one of them, there was a person who was victim of his own frustration in his pursuit towards inexistent perfection.

With all the people that I have met and that have come here to share their stories with us, Greg my dear wise spirit, it is clear that everyone has a life story that includes happy times and sad times. We are all wounded in some way, trying to heal and figure it out.

We need some compassion . . .